Isadora Duncan

by Joanne Mattern

 HOUGHTON MIFFLIN   BOSTON

PHOTOGRAPHY CREDITS: Cover © Lebrecht Music & Arts/The Image Works; tp © Underwood & Underwood/ Corbis; 2 © Thomas Northcut/Getty Images; 4, 5 © Print Collector/HIP/The Image Works; 6 © Greek/Getty Images; 7 © Lebrecht Music & Arts/The Image Works; 8 © Mary Evans Picture Library/The Image Works; 9 © Getty Images; 10 © Corbis; 11 © Time & Life Pictures/Getty Images; 12–13 © Underwood & Underwood/CORBIS; 14 © Scott Indermaur Photography, Inc./Workbook Stock/Jupiter Images.

Printed in China

ISBN-13: 978-0-547-02178-2
ISBN-10: 0-547-02178-X

14 15 16 17 0940 19 18 17 16
4500569761

What do you do when you feel happy? Do you jump up and down? Maybe you twirl and dance. You might want to sing a happy song.

People can show their feelings by the way they express themselves. Artists may paint pictures while performers may dance, sing, or play music.

It's hard not to smile when you sing!

✦ A New Dance ✦

Ballet has been a popular kind of dance for many years. A ballet dancer uses a specific kind of movement in the steps of a dance to express emotion or to tell a story.

About one hundred years ago, a woman named Isadora Duncan wanted to create a new kind of dance. It was hard to change people's minds about what a dance should look like, but Isadora wouldn't let other people's doubts stop her dreams. She helped create a style called modern dance that has changed dance forever.

✦ A Star Is Born ✦

Angela Isadora Duncan was born in San Francisco, California, in 1878. She was the youngest of four children.

The Duncan family did not have much money. However, Isadora's mother was a pianist and felt it was important for her children to learn about and enjoy the arts.

Isadora often performed wearing white robes.

As a result, Isadora was able to study ballet. She was so good that by the age of six she was already teaching younger children how to dance.

✦ Isadora Pursues Her Dream ✦

In 1895, Isadora and her mother moved east so that she could pursue her dancing career. One of her first performances was as a fairy in *A Midsummer Night's Dream*, a very famous play and ballet. Eventually, she joined a dance company and performed in many ballets.

In 1897, the dance company went to London, England, where Isadora made her European debut.

Isadora's dance moves were different from other dancers in the 1890's.

Isadora met a lot of artists in London who taught her many things. Isadora especially liked learning about ancient Greece. She thought that Greek statues of women were very beautiful, and she loved the simple flowing dresses that they wore. Isadora began to wear this type of Greek dress as a costume when she danced.

Isadora wore dancing clothes similar to the robes she saw on Greek statues.

✦ Sharing the Dance ✦

In addition to performing on stage, Isadora also gave private performances in people's homes. She often danced barefoot. She also skipped and ran instead of using the formal steps of ballet. Isadora based each movement on her feelings.

People were fascinated with this new style of dancing, and Isadora became very popular.

Isadora didn't need shoes for her dances!

Isadora worked hard with her students.

✦ Teaching the Dance to Others ✦

Isadora wanted to share her dance with others. So, in 1904, she opened a dance school for young girls. Eventually, she also opened schools in France and Russia.

Isadora's students learned to move to the rhythm of the music and to move gracefully. Most importantly, they learned that simple movements could become beautiful dances.

✦ Dancing in the United States ✦

In 1908, Isadora left Europe to tour the United States. People were used to ballet dancers who wore fancy costumes. They liked huge performances that involved large pieces of scenery and many dancers. They did not understand Isadora's simple, free style. As a result, some people did not like her performances.

Isadora was very graceful.

President Theodore Roosevelt was a big fan of Isadora's.

Isadora did not let people's negative reactions upset her. She did not need their permission to dance the way she wanted.

However, President Theodore Roosevelt said Isadora's dancing made him think of a child in a beautiful garden. People liked that idea. They began to understand and appreciate Isadora. President Roosevelt helped make Isadora's trip to the United States a triumph.

✦ The Isadorables ✦

Isadora's fame began to spread like wildfire to many countries. She danced all over the world, often performing with her students. These girls were called "The Isadorables."

Then, in 1913, a terrible thing happened. Isadora's two children drowned. She was so mournful after this that she did not want to dance anymore.

Isadora wanted her students to look like ancient Greeks, too!

After a while, Isadora missed dancing, and she returned to the stage. She used dance to express her sadness and her joy. People now loved the new ideas that she brought to the dance world. Her fame towered above other dancers.

Isadora and her students continued to dance in Europe and the United States. Their audiences grew larger.

Isadora and her students performing in 1918.

⋆ A Dance That ⋆ Changed the World

Isadora wanted her style of dance to live on forever. Teaching other dancers was very important to her and some of her students became dance teachers too. It was this dancing tradition that helped Isadora change the world of dance.

★ The Birth of Modern Dance ★

Isadora Duncan died in 1927. By then, modern dance had been born. Like Isadora, modern dancers use natural movements to express joy, sorrow, and other powerful feelings.

The little girl who loved to dance grew up to be one of the greatest dancers in the world!

Modern Dance Today

Today, modern dance does not have just one style. People who create modern dance include all different kinds of movements and music. This is an art form that is always changing.

Just like in Isadora's time, people often learn ballet if they want to perfom modern dance.

Responding

✔ **TARGET SKILL** **Author's Purpose** What is the author's purpose for writing this story? What details does she use to support her purpose? Copy and complete the chart below.

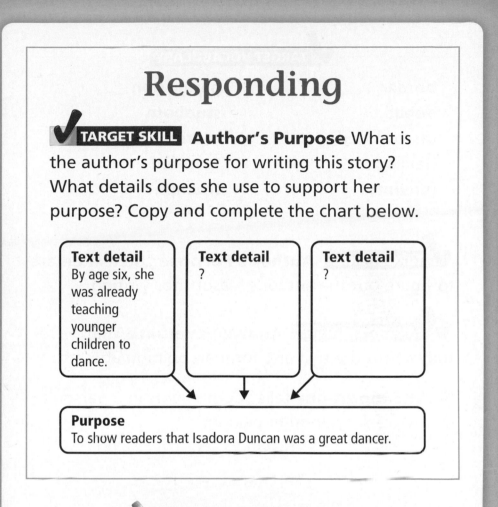

Text detail
By age six, she was already teaching younger children to dance.

Text detail
?

Text detail
?

Purpose
To show readers that Isadora Duncan was a great dancer.

Write About It

Text to Self Think of someone you admire. Write a paragraph explaining why you admire this person. Be sure to include specific details that support why you chose this person.

border	permission
debut	stubborn
discouraged	toured
hauling	towered
mournful	triumph

✓ **TARGET SKILL** **Author's Purpose** Use text details to figure out the author's reasons for writing.

✓ **TARGET STRATEGY** **Analyze/Evaluate** Think carefully about the text and form an opinion about it.

GENRE Biography tells about events in a person's life, written by another person.